St. Mary's Osterley playgroup

HEDGEHOGS

Joanne Jessop

Nature Study

Ants
Bees and Wasps
Birds of Prey
Butterflies and Moths
Frogs and Toads

Hedgehogs
Rabbits and Hares
Snakes and Lizards
Spiders
Worms

Cover: A hedgehog among ivy leaves.

Frontispiece: A hedgehog looking for worms in damp soil.

This book is based on an original text by Elizabeth Bomford.

First published in 1990 by
Wayland (Publishers) Limited
61 Western Road, Hove,
East Sussex BN3 1JD, England

© Copyright 1990 Wayland (Publishers) Limited

Editor: Alison Cooper
Series editor: Sue Hadden

British Library Cataloguing in Publication Data
Jessop, Joanne
  Hedgehogs.
  1. Hedgehogs
  I. Title
  599.3′3

ISBN 1–85210–888–6

Typeset by Kalligraphics Ltd, Horley, Surrey.
Printed in Turin, Italy by G.Canale and C.S.p.A.
Bound in France by A.G.M.

Contents

Words printed in **bold** are explained in the glossary.

Introducing hedgehogs

A hedgehog is a small **mammal** with prickles on the back of its head and body. If it is frightened, a hedgehog curls up tightly, so that the soft parts of its body are on the inside. Few enemies can get at a hedgehog when it is curled up.

There are lots of different kinds of hedgehog. They live in Britain and the rest of Europe, right across to the USSR and East China. In the hot, dry areas of Africa and Asia there are

This hedgehog is looking for food.

   ➔ This is a desert hedgehog from Morocco.

desert hedgehogs. They dig burrows to get away from the hot sun and to hide from their enemies.

    Not all animals that look like hedgehogs belong to the same family. Porcupines and the Australian spiny anteater have prickles on their backs but they do not belong to the same family as the hedgehog.

What hedgehogs look like

The hedgehog's spines, or prickles, are like stiff hairs. Each spine is about 22 mm long. Older hedgehogs have more spines than younger ones. A young hedgehog's spines are shiny and in good condition, but the spines of an old hedgehog are often damaged.

A hedgehog uses a special set of **muscles** to raise and lower its prickles. When it is frightened, a hedgehog tightens the muscles around its sides. This is how it curls up. A hedgehog can stay curled up for a long time without getting tired.

◀ A hedgehog's spines look like this.

▲ Can you see this hedgehog's eyes and its pointed snout?

A hedgehog's small bright eyes are not very good at seeing things. A hedgehog uses its good sense of smell and hearing to find its way around.

How hedgehogs live

Hedgehogs live on their own. If they are with another hedgehog, it is usually because they are sharing a feeding area, such as a lawn.

This hedgehog is looking for food along a garden wall.

◆ Hedgehogs feed on lawns because the short grass makes it easy to find worms.

Like most mammals, hedgehogs have their own special smell. The hedgehog's smell is quite strong. A hedgehog can tell the age of another hedgehog by its smell, and whether it is a male or a female. Usually a hedgehog's smell warns other hedgehogs to keep out of its way. But during the **mating** season, hedgehogs use their smell to find a mate.

Town and country hedgehogs

During the day, hedgehogs sleep in small nests under bushes or among the roots of trees. At night they come out to look for food.

Hedgehogs live in places that have plenty of shelter as well as food. Meadows surrounded by hedges make good places for hedgehogs to live. They also live on the edges of woods. Sometimes they feed in damp places along the banks of streams.

◀ Hedgehogs like to sleep among tree roots.

Hedgehogs are not shy of people, and many hedgehogs live in gardens in towns. Sometimes a hedgehog will come to the door to be fed and become almost a family pet. ▶

◀ Hedgehogs can swim across small ponds.

What hedgehogs eat

Finding food in the wild

Earthworms are a hedgehog's favourite food. You can often see hedgehogs hunting at night in parks and on golf courses and lawns. They can find worms easily in these places because the grass is short.

This hedgehog is looking for earthworms.

When it is hunting, a hedgehog walks slowly, turning its head from side to side and snuffling gently.

When the weather is dry, earthworms stay deep in the soil, so hedgehogs hunt for slugs, caterpillars and frogs instead. During the early spring, hungry hedgehogs often attack the nests of mice and voles to eat their young.

Hedgehogs also eat the grubs of craneflies, which attack carrots and turnips. In this way hedgehogs help farmers and gardeners.

In dry weather, hedgehogs ▶ eat slugs.

Finding food in the town

The hedgehogs that live in towns find food in many different places. In gardens they eat worms, slugs and snails. Sometimes, they go to rubbish tips to look for a meal.

Hedgehogs also look for food in picnic areas. But this can be dangerous for them. A hedgehog might try to lick out the last few sweet drops from a plastic cup that has been left behind after a picnic. The cup may get stuck on its head.

➤ Hedgehogs sometimes eat food put out for cats and dogs.

▲ Hedgehogs can eat eggs from hens' nests.

A hedgehog can usually break a plastic cup and free itself. But if a hedgehog gets stuck in a tin can, it may die, because it cannot break a tin can.

Staying alive

Curling up and fighting back

An adult hedgehog has between 5,000 and 7,000 sharp spines on its back. When a hedgehog is curled up in a tight ball, the criss-cross of prickles stops other animals from getting at the hedgehog. There are many animals that would eat a hedgehog if they could get it to uncurl.

This fox cub is trying to make a hedgehog uncurl. ▶

➤ When a hedgehog curls up, it looks like a prickly ball.

Sometimes hedgehogs use their prickles to attack animals that are bothering them. Instead of curling up tight, the hedgehog stands still and waits for the animal to get really close. Then the hedgehog jumps up quickly and sticks its spines into the animal's nose. This is very painful and may explain why a lot of animals leave hedgehogs alone!

Hedgehogs in danger

Most people like hedgehogs because they are harmless creatures. But **gamekeepers** often kill hedgehogs because they eat pheasant and partridge eggs.

➤ This young hedgehog has uncurled after rolling down a log.

Gardeners like to have a hedgehog living in the vegetable patch because it eats many garden **pests.** But gardeners who use poisons to kill pests may also kill hedgehogs by accident. A hedgehog may die if it eats the poison or if it eats an animal that has eaten the poison.

◀ Hedgehogs eat slugs and lots of other pests, like the snail shown below. ➡

▲ Many hedgehogs are killed on roads.

A hedgehog can curl up to protect itself from other animals.
But curling up does not protect it from cars and lawn mowers.
Many hedgehogs are killed on the roads each year because
they do not get out of the way of cars in time.

Hedgehogs hiding in long grass are sometimes killed by lawn mowers. The machines used to cut the plants that grow alongside country roads often kill hedgehogs too.

➤ Country roadsides would be much safer places for hedgehogs to live if the grass and wild flowers were left to grow.

Hedgehog families

When a female is ready to mate, her smell changes. Male hedgehogs pick up her scent and start to look for her. The first male to find her behaves in a special way. He moves around the female in circles, making a snorting noise. He may have to do this for several hours. He is trying to get the female to lower her spines so that he can mate with her.

➡ The male hedgehog is trying to make the female lower her spines.

➤ These hedgehogs are mating.

Sometimes more than one male wants to mate with the same female. When this happens, the male hedgehogs fight each other. Sometimes the female wanders away while the males are fighting. After a male and female have mated, the male takes no more interest in the female.

▲ This hedgehog is asleep in its nest.

About three weeks after mating, a female hedgehog builds a nest in a safe place at the bottom of a hedge or under some brambles. Four and a half weeks after mating, the female gives birth. There are usually four or five baby hedgehogs in a **litter.**

When they are born, baby hedgehogs are pink and their prickles are covered with a white skin. This skin protects the mother from the baby's prickles during the birth.

A newborn hedgehog is blind and helpless. A few hours after a hedgehog is born, white prickles begin to poke through its skin. As the hedgehog grows, dark spines appear.

▼ This baby hedgehog's eyes have not opened yet.

▲ This hedgehog is three weeks old. It is in the nest.

Baby hedgehogs suck milk from their mother. When the baby hedgehogs are about three weeks old, the mother takes them on short trips away from the nest. They learn how to hunt for food by watching their mother.

◄ Baby hedgehogs soon learn to find food for themselves.

When the baby hedgehogs are between four and six weeks old, the mother raises her prickles so that the baby hedgehogs cannot feed from her milk. Then the hedgehogs leave their mother and begin to live on their own.

Surviving in the winter

Hedgehogs eat as much as they can during the summer and autumn, when there is lots of food about. They grow bigger and fatter.

➤ During the summer and autumn, hedgehogs eat lots of food.

▲ This young hedgehog has woken up to look for food in the winter snow.

There is not much food for animals in the winter. In cold weather, they need food to keep their bodies warm. If a hedgehog tried to look for food during the winter months, it would not be able to find enough to keep it warm. It would die of cold. So hedgehogs **hibernate** during the winter. They live off the fat they have stored in their bodies during the summer.

▲ A hedgehog's winter nest.

A hedgehog prepares for hibernation by making a winter nest. It makes a pile of leaves and grass. Then it rolls around inside the pile, using its prickles to shape the nest.

The winter nest is much thicker than the nest that the hedgehog makes to sleep in during the day.

Hibernation is more than just a deep sleep. When a hedgehog hibernates, its body temperature falls. Its heartbeat slows down. It breathes only once every few minutes and it looks as if it is dead. The hedgehog does not need any food. Its fat keeps it alive during the cold winter months.

▲ A hedgehog will stay awake during the winter if there is lots of food for it to eat.

Some young hedgehogs are not fat enough to hibernate for the whole winter. If you see a hedgehog during the winter, give it some food. This may save its life. When it has eaten enough it will go back to sleep.

Learning more about hedgehogs

Watching hedgehogs

A good place to look for hedgehogs is a playing field. Get an adult to take you there at night, when hedgehogs come out of their nests to look for food. You must be very quiet because a hedgehog will run away if it hears a noise.

➤ If you frighten a hedgehog, it will curl up to protect itself.

▲ This hedgehog is sniffing through autumn leaves, looking for worms.

On a warm, damp summer's night, when there are lots of earthworms near the surface of the soil, you may see several hedgehogs sniffing for food.

Looking after hedgehogs

It is not a good idea to take a wild hedgehog home with you to keep as a pet. It might be a mother hedgehog with a litter of young ones hidden in a bush. Without their mother, the baby hedgehogs will die. But you may find a sick or injured hedgehog that you want to care for.

➥ Hedgehogs do not usually come out in the sun. Perhaps this hedgehog is sick.

▲ Hedgehogs sometimes make good pets.

In the late autumn and winter, there may be some young hedgehogs that are too little to stay alive during the winter hibernation. You can sometimes take care of these young hedgehogs for a few months. A hedgehog that is getting plenty of food may not hibernate but this will not harm it.

Do not keep a pet hedgehog in the house, as they are very messy. The best place to keep a hedgehog is in a garden shed.

You will need to give your pet hedgehog food and water every day. It will also need some hay to make a nest.

Hedgehogs need plenty of **protein.** Feed your hedgehog a mixture of meat scraps, vegetables and potatoes. Some hedgehogs like eggs too.

Hedgehogs are covered with fleas. These are special hedgehog fleas that do not like humans at all.

➡ This is a hedgehog flea on a pinhead.

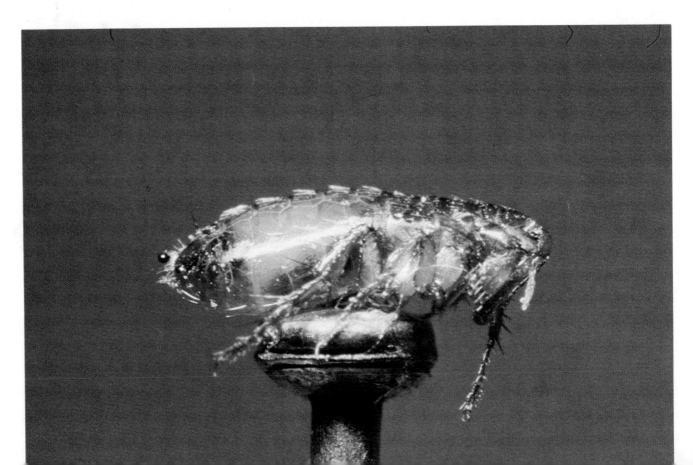

▲ This hedgehog is spreading saliva over its body.

Hedgehogs have a very strange habit. When a hedgehog smells certain things, for example boot polish, it throws itself on the ground and covers its back and sides with **saliva.** No one knows why hedgehogs do this.

Hedgehog myths

There are many **myths** about hedgehogs. In one old story hedgehogs carry fallen apples away from an orchard by sticking them on their spines. Today we know that hedgehogs do not often eat fruit.

➡ This woman is trying to find out if hedgehogs can carry apples on their spines.

People used to believe stories that told how hedgehogs could suck milk from cows. Hedgehogs like milk, and perhaps people believed these stories because they often saw hedgehogs near cow sheds.

Glossary

Gamekeepers   People who look after game birds, for example, pheasants, on country estates.

Hibernate   To sleep during the winter.

Litter   A group of baby animals born at the same time to the same mother.

Mammal   A warm-blooded animal with hair or fur. Mammals feed their babies on their milk.

Mating   When a male and female animal pair to produce babies.

Muscles   Parts of an animal's body that give it the power and strength to move.

Myths   Stories from long ago that people believed were true.

Pests   Insects that destroy crops.

Protein   A substance found in many foods. It is needed for healthy growth.

Saliva   The liquid produced in the mouth. It is also called spit.

Finding out more

If you would like to find out more about hedgehogs, you might like to read some of these books.

The Handbook of British Mammals G. B. Corbett & H. N. Southern (Blackwell, 1977)
The Hedgehog Joyce Pope (Hamish Hamilton, 1985)
Hedgehogs Liz Bomford (A. & C. Black, 1986)
Prickly Orphans Ann Williams (Macdonald, 1987)

Index

Picture Acknowledgements

All photographs are by Elizabeth Bomford, except p.9 (Bruce Coleman: M. Gunthe/O. Langrand) and cover (Oxford Scientific Films: Tim Shepherd).